Studies in Musical Science & Philosophy
Vol 2

Piano Unison Tuning

Brian Capleton PhD

Adaptations from published papers

Dr Brian Capleton lectured in Piano Technology at the Royal National College, and is an alumnus of Wolfson College Oxford, the Royal College of Music, Trinity College of Music London, and Dartington College of Arts.

Published by Amarilli Books

Copyright © 2015, Brian Capleton

1st Edition

ISBN 978-0-9928141-7-5

A CIP catalogue record for this book is available
from the British Library.

Contents

The Background

Piano tuning is an art whose techniques are closely related to acoustical science. The underlying science for the practical approach is based on a what is essentially a nineteenth century theoretical model, and it is this "traditional" theory that provides the ground principles trainee tuners must put into practice in the learning process.

Empirical experience, however, soon reveals to observant tuners many of the limitations of "traditional" theory applied to the modern instrument. More advanced tuners soon become aware that in practice there is a great deal more to learn in the practical art, even just regarding the techniques, on which the "traditional" theory has little or nothing to say.

The "traditional" theory deals primarily with a theoretically calculated method for the tuning of the equally tempered scale (a scale with "equal sized" semitones). It can easily be misunderstood from the emphasis of the theory, that achieving equal temperament as a series of string frequencies or pitches, is what the art of piano tuning is all about.

Whilst the creation of "equal temperament" is a necessary part of piano tuning - and one that is indeed not as straightforward as musicians might assume – for the expert tuner it is nevertheless only one dimension of the task, and it certainly does not represent the challenge or art of tuning as a whole.

On the one hand the "traditional" theory gives the impression that the practical art of piano tuning can be described as a straightforward theoretical problem about musical interval sizes and string frequencies, to which there is an involved, but nevertheless straightforward technical answer.

On the other hand, adept tuners know that whilst the tuning of "equally tempered" interval sizes is a necessary part of the process, piano tuning is overall an art of tone and intonation production, through the tuning of unisons, intervals, and the relative tuning over the whole compass.

Tuning and tone are closely connected. "Traditional" piano tuning theory is based on the idealised principles of *temperament theory*, and taken at face value it can lead to the tacit assumption that fine tone production must simply follow from the practical application of these principles.

In fact the theory says nothing about positive tone production, and deals only with the elimination of basically undesirable tonal qualities, and the application of tempering principles. The reality is that far from being a definitive description of the art of piano tuning, "traditional" theory actually fails to describe many of the most important and critical processes in which master tuners are continually involved.

It is practical experience rather than the "traditional" theory, that teaches the true complexity and variability of the piano's tuning characteristics, how to control piano tone, how to balance one part of the compass with another, and how to work with tone as a sonic medium to bring a given instrument to its optimum condition.

For the discerning musician (and others including audiophiles and recording engineers), beauty of tone is not a theoretical concept entirely encapsulated by a scientific definition. It is a practical reality brought into being by the instrument, the pianist, and to an equally important extent by the piano tuner. The extent to which the tuner can enhance or fail the tonal potential of an instrument is perhaps something not as widely appreciated as it could be.

There is not a straightforward theoretical answer to the relationship between tuning and tone. A common misconception is that the "answer" to the "problem" of piano tuning, lies in a "correct" set of frequencies for the notes.

In actuality, every note consists of a very large number of frequencies, many of which may be unstable, and all of which are only one kind of ingredient, or parameter, in a constantly changing, complex recipe. Expert tuners do not use their hearing and techniques in the attempt to create a set of frequencies. Rather, their hearing and specialist techniques are used to produce tone, whilst the actual relationship between tuning, tone and frequency, remains very complex.

Misconceptions about this arise as much in the professional training ground as outside it. This begins with "traditional" theory. The theory calculates, from an assumed set of frequencies, a set of audible *beat rates* for the tempered intervals. This makes it look as though tuning by beats is a technique for producing the assumed theoretical frequencies.

In fact, beats are a critical and unavoidable part of tone, and hence part of the overall subject of tone production. In expert tuning, beats are controlled, so to speak, for their own sake, or for the sake of the effect they have on tone and intonation, and not for the purpose of producing specific string frequencies.

The beginnings of tone control do necessarily lie in learning to control *beat phenomena* in the audible soundscape, so the learner spends a great deal of time intensively involved in controlling this beat phenomena according to the theoretical guidelines.

This, in turn, misleadingly suggests that tuning is all about *beating* or its absence, as an artefact. Many students invariably reach a point at which all they "hear" is beating, out of its true context which is musical tone and intonation.

One small but important area in which the underlying acoustical complexity behind tone reveals itself, is in the tuning of trichord unisons, which are the piano's groups of three strings to one note. In "traditional" piano tuning parlance the process of tuning a unison is very crudely and somewhat dismissively referred to as "tuning out the beat".

In actuality the fine tuning region of a unison is, for the artist tuner, a region in which the *tone* of the unison is finely controlled. This tone is determined by many parameters that cannot be reduced simply to the concept of "beating" or "no beating". The perceived tone can even be affected by psycho-acoustic factors.

There is no one single, "archetypal" unison tone or tuning behaviour for all piano unisons, as the "traditional" model suggests. Pianos vary greatly in their tuning characteristics, and in the ways in which tone control of the unisons is possible. Variation takes place from one part of the compass to another, from note to note, from piano to piano, and is dependent on the make, size, age and condition of the piano.

Because most of the piano's compass consists of notes having unison groups (or pairs) of strings, the unison is the basic "building block" of the instrument's tone. To be sure, how these building blocks are put together is also a critical feature of the overall tonal and musical qualities of an instrument.

Nevertheless, the quality of unison tuning itself, that can be created by the acoustical "materials" inherent in a given piano, is a matter of considerably more art and expertise than the concept of "tuning out the beat" can represent.

This is not so surprising when it is recognised that the unison can contain *multiple* beats, fluctuations that are not genuine repeating beat patterns, and decaying partials whose decay rates can be as important as beat rates.

Whilst the practical art of tone production is sometimes best discussed using the language of art, and whilst tonal beauty may not even be a suitable subject for scientific scrutiny, there still remains a relationship between the art and scientific descriptions, mainly because the medium of this art is musical sound.

The sound associated with piano tone is complex, but also happens to be structured in a way that lends itself well to scientific analysis. Consequently, modern acoustical theory can go a great deal further than "traditional" theory in at least revealing the general kinds of processes in which expert tuners are empirically involved. Some of these processes may remain relatively inscrutable if they are fundamentally ones of artistic discernment, but much of what takes place even in empirical judgement, is nevertheless prompted or limited by the physics of the instrument.

This article endeavours to show a little of how contemporary science approaches this one small but important part of what the expert tuner does in practice – the tuning of unisons.

Unisons on the piano

Over most of the piano's compass, a single piano note is comprised of three strings - a *trichord* or *unison group*. Roughly speaking, we could say all three strings have to be tuned "to the same note", but expert piano tuners know very well that in practice there is far more to tuning the unison trichord than this.

The idea of tuning a musical "note" at a given "pitch" is itself highly over-simplistic when it comes to the practical realities of piano tuning. The concept of a musical "note" at a particular "pitch" is useful in music theory and music practice, but is not very useful for understanding the nature of tone, or how the tone of the piano unison group is affected by the relative tuning between the strings.

Musical pitch – some myths

The very concept of musical *pitch* can itself be most misleading. Many musicians (and non musicians) naturally feel that *pitch* is some entirely objective property of musical sound. If this were the case, then it would be quantitatively measurable, and indeed it is often spoken about just as if it were.

In fact, contrary to this intuitive view, there is no scientific unit of pitch, because pitch is a subjective sensory response, rather than an objective, measurable property of sound. There are two measurables in acoustics that are often mistaken for scientific units of pitch, or pitch differences. These measurables are the Hertz, or cycle per second, and the *cent*, which is often described as 1/100th of an equally tempered semitone.

Firstly, *frequency* (the number of vibrations or cycles per second, measured in Hertz) is associated with *pitch* because sound waves with different frequencies are generally perceived at different pitches. This association does not, however, mean that frequency is a measurement of pitch.

It is perfectly possible for one frequency to be perceived at a number of different pitches, depending on the context, the loudness, and the perceiving individual. In the case of *binaural diplacusis* a given frequency may even be perceived at a different pitch in each ear of the same person.

Two individual sound wave frequencies within a certain range, are commonly perceived as being separated by a recognisable musical interval if their frequencies are in certain ratios. There are natural acoustical reasons (rather than Pythagorean, mystical reasons) why this is so. Certain, simple whole number ratios between certain frequencies, produce for many listeners, recognisable musical intervals.

Ratios, and in particular *frequency ratios*, can therefore be associated with perceived musical intervals. Simple ratios associated with musical intervals can also appear between the speaking lengths of musical strings. For example, when a guitar string is stopped at half its length, its pitch rises an octave.

Similar ratios are found between the lengths of pipes and their notes. In no case, however, does the *association* of musical intervals with these physical ratios, mean that the Hertz or the metre or the foot are themselves *scientific units* for the measurement of pitch or pitch difference.

The cent

A calculated ratio for the modern (equally tempered) semitone interval is $2^{1/12} : 1$. This is a ratio derived from the ratio associated with the octave, which is 2:1. The octave is, so to speak, mathematically "sliced" into 12 equal semitones. From the semitone ratio is then calculated a micro-interval ratio for an interval a hundred times smaller, called the *cent*. This has a value of $2^{1/1200} : 1$. The cent is a ratio, usually applied to *frequencies*, that is sometimes used to give an intuitive indication of the relative sizes of musical intervals, or more loosely, of hypothetical micro-differences in pitch.

However, because the cent is not an actual unit of pitch or pitch difference, a statement such as, for example, "we must measure pitch to an accuracy of 0.001 cents" is scientifically ambiguous or even meaningless. A more reliable and meaningful statement would be "we must measure *frequency ratio* to an accuracy of 0.001 cents".

Perceived pitch itself is not something that can be rigorously expressed in thousandths of a cent. The relationship between such a precise measurement in cents, and actual perceived pitch, is far more fluid, complicated, and unreliable than the precision of the measurement suggests. Such precision can only be properly applied to frequency ratios, or other ratios between scientific measurables with recognised units.

Beyond pitch

The question then naturally arises, what *is* the relationship between frequency and pitch? The answer is that the relationship is complex, variable, and also subject to psycho-acoustic factors. In particular, most musical tones are not single frequencies. In the case of a single piano string, its tone is a mixture of a large number of different frequencies.

This set of frequencies consists of a *fundamental* or lowest frequency, plus a considerable number of higher frequencies present in other *partials*.[1] No one of those frequencies alone, in general, completely determines the perceived pitch. Although the fundamental "corresponds" to the perceived pitch, the other partials also affect the pitch. Furthermore, perceived pitch depends also on a number of parameters other than frequency.[2]

Pitch is only one aspect of musical tone. The notion that piano tuners are tuning unison strings "to the same pitch", may be coincidentally true in simple, colloquial, musical terms, but it does not reflect what the tuning process is all about, or how the tone of the unison is related to the fine

---

[1] Around middle C on a reasonably good piano, there are typically in excess of 20 partials that show up above the noise floor in digital analysis, using standard equipment.

[2] A good introductory account of pitch dependency can be found in Campbell, M, & Greated, C, *The musician's guide to acoustics*, London, 1987.

tuning condition. "Equality" of pitch is relatively easily achieved, whilst excellent and consistent tone quality is not.

Even the "traditional" nineteenth century theory, being a scientific theory concerned with the objective acoustics, does not deal with pitch, but with frequency. In "traditional" theory there is no important issue here - the three unison strings are simply tuned to the same tension, and they have the same lowest frequency. As far as "traditional" theory is concerned, the relative tuning between the strings is zero, so there is nothing more to say about it.

The actuality is that the relative fine tuning of the strings of the trichord is most important in piano tuning, precisely because it controls the fine tone of the unisons, which not only contributes to the tones of the other intervals, but collectively accumulates to contribute to the tone of the instrument as a whole. Contemporary acoustics, in contrast, is able to show why we should not necessarily expect a truly zero relative tuning between the strings.

The "traditional string"

In order to put "traditional" theory into perspective we have to begin with "traditional" theory itself. "Traditional" piano tuning theory begins with a theoretical model for the vibrating piano string.

The model is a relatively simple one of the kind found in standard undergraduate text books on vibrations and waves. The string itself is regarded as perfectly flexible and is considered as vibrating in one plane, between two rigid boundaries (the bridges) at the ends of the string's speaking length.

The vibration on a string is caused by waves travelling along the string and reflecting off the boundaries at the ends. The resulting waves travelling in opposite directions along the string, combine to produce *standing wave* motion as the vibration of the string.

A single string can support a large number of standing waves of different wavelengths and frequencies, but only certain wavelengths can occur, determined by the speaking length of the string. The frequencies produced by a string in the model of "traditional" theory, consequently fall into a set known as the *harmonic series*, in which the lowest frequency is the *fundamental* frequency, and all other frequencies generated are whole number multiples of the fundamental frequency.

All the frequencies occur simultaneously, and together form a *recipe* for the overall complicated motion of the string. This motion's energy is then transmitted to soundboard which in turn radiates the sound we hear.

Each individual frequency within the overall recipe of string motion is similarly responsible for producing an individual audible *harmonic*. The theory then presumes all the harmonics mixed together are heard as the overall tone of the string, radiated from the soundboard.

Real piano strings produce a set of audible "overtones" that are the "real version" of "traditional" theory's hypothetical *harmonics*. Piano tuners today usually call these *partials*. They can be easily isolated on a bass string of a grand piano, by touching the string at any position that would divide the speaking length into whole number proportions, and then playing the note.

The fundamental cannot be isolated very well, but touching the string half way along its speaking length will produce a clear second partial, or touching 1/3 along the length will produce the 3rd partial, and so on.

Limitations of the "traditional" model

This elementary model has a number of important limitations. Probably the most widely appreciated is the fact that real piano strings are far from being perfectly flexible. This produces the now well known effect called *inharmonicity*, in which the frequencies produced do not fall perfectly in the harmonic series (they are no longer perfectly whole number multiples of the fundamental).

Although it is a complicating factor, the effects of inharmonicity to reasonable accuracy, can be relatively easily predicted, and treated, so to speak, as an "add on" to the basic theory. There are, however, other important limitations that will not yield so easily to this kind of "add on" treatment.

The first of these is the fact that at one end of the string's speaking length is the soundboard bridge, which is not designed to be an acoustically rigid boundary. The bridge is designed to move a little, in order to transmit energy from the string motion to the soundboard, which having a larger surface area than the string, acts as an amplifier that radiates sound waves into the air. The effect of the movable bridge is twofold.

The bridge has two different physical properties that affect its motion. The first is its elastic or "spring like" property together with its inertial or "mass-like" property, which is known as its *reactive* component. The reactive component has (amongst other effects) the effect of changing each wave frequency slightly, depending on the bridge's reactive value at that particular frequency.

The second property of the bridge is its *dissipative* or *resistive* component, which is "friction like" and has the main effect of draining energy away from the string, causing the characteristic *decay* or "dying away" of the string's motion, and consequently of the sound heard.

Another important limitation connected with the last one, is that in practice the string does not simply vibrate in one plane only. Vibration in one plane only would mean the string was in a state of *planar polarisation*, which in theory can happen, but is not the general case. Planar polarisation is a special, limited instance of the more general polarisation state: elliptical polarisation.

Piano strings are perfectly capable of supporting elliptically polarised wave motion other than planar polarisation, but, as it turns out, they cannot even be assumed to be in a stable, fixed state of elliptical polarisation. Put more simply, piano strings may be struck in one plane by the hammer, but they end up vibrating in another plane, or in more than one plane, and the planes themselves may move.

Arguably the most important limitation, is that in practice all three strings of the unison group lie side by side on the same moving soundboard bridge, which means the motion of the three strings is connected. As a whole, the unison is a *coupled* vibrational system. Coupled oscillator systems are a well known phenomenon in physics and acoustics. They are in general capable of much more complicated motion than individual, uncoupled oscillators.

Lastly, the sound we hear is not primarily the sound radiated by the string motion itself, but rather, is that radiated by the soundboard motion, which is subject a further set of influences.

The "traditional" view of the unison

The "traditional" theory's unison consists of three hypothetical strings that are treated as acoustically isolated from each other. Each string produces its own set of audible harmonics.

Since for each string, the frequencies of its harmonics are whole number multiples of its fundamental frequency, the theory says that all we have to do is make the fundamental frequencies of all three strings the same, and then the harmonics produced by the three strings will also be the same frequency at each position in the series.

We can liken the "harmonic series" produced by the string to the rungs on a vertical ladder, where the lowest rung represents the fundamental (harmonic number 1), and the next rung up is harmonic number 2, and so on. The three strings of a trichord unison would then be represented by three ladders, side by side. As long as the lowest rungs, or fundamentals, of all three ladders are aligned, then *all* the rungs will be aligned, provided the ladders are identical.

"Aligning" harmonics is important because two harmonics that are not quite aligned will together produce audible *beating* – a "vibrato-like" effect in the partial. If they are close in frequency (but not the same) they will be aurally indistinguishable as separate harmonics, and rather, will be heard as a single partial that fluctuates up and down in loudness, or *beats*.

Too much beating makes the unison sound "out of tune" and spoils the tone. A "perfectly" tuned unison in "traditional" theory would therefore be one in which there is perfect alignment between all the harmonics, or ladder rungs, and no beating.

The three unison strings are then equivalent to three identical ladders placed on the same level, so all the rungs align perfectly. Mistuning one string would be like raising or lowering the level of one ladder, and changing its rung spacing, so that there was misalignment between its rungs and the rungs of the other ladders.

There is in this model a simple relationship between the mistuning between two strings, and the rapidity of the audible beating. The *beat rate*, as piano tuners call it, is the number of beats per second.

The beat rate is simply equal to the mistuning between the two "misaligned" frequencies responsible for the beat. Two harmonics at frequencies 256 Hz and 257 Hz, for example, will beat together with a beat rate of 1 beat per second, the same as the mistuning or difference between the two frequencies.

Inharmonicity, perhaps the best known of the complications that occur in the real situation, is not so difficult to incorporate into this picture. Inharmonicity, as already said, is a raising of the harmonics from their proper harmonic series frequencies.

In the ladder analogy it would cause a raising of the position of each rung, but the nature of inharmonicity is that the higher the rung, the more it is raised above its normal position.

This would make the ladders somewhat more difficult to climb, the higher one climbed, but a little consideration will reveal that as long as the "inharmonicity" on each ladder is identical, inharmonicity will still allow all the rungs to be aligned. In other words, in real piano strings, inharmonicity is not an intrinsic problem in tuning the unison, provided the three strings are identical in their inharmonicity.

In this "traditional" view of the unison, it is therefore said that unisons are tuned to a "zero beating" condition, by placing the fundamental frequencies of all three strings to the same value. Even in this elementary model, it should be remembered if a "mistuning" exists between the strings, and beating occurs, it is not a single beat pattern that occurs.

It is, rather, multiple beat patterns that occur, because "mistuning" between the fundamentals (or a misaligning of the lowest rungs), will result in a mistuning at every "harmonic" position in the series (at every rung), and hence beating will occur at every position in the "harmonic" series (all the rungs would mis-align).

The edict from "traditional" theory then, is simply to "eliminate the beating", and the unison will be considered tuned. Importantly, if we were to measure the fundamental frequencies of the strings, we would by this theory then find them to be the same. Provided the strings are identical, this principle in "traditional" theory remains true *even when inharmonicity is taken into account.*

Harmonics and partials

Piano tuners often speak of listening to *partials*, rather than harmonics. This is rightly so, firstly because the word *harmonic* only refers to a frequency that is a whole number multiple of the fundamental, or lowest frequency.

Because piano strings are stiff and inharmonic, they produce frequencies that are not perfectly whole number multiples of the fundamental, so these frequency components have to be referred to as partials rather than harmonics.

This is the "usual" understanding of the difference between harmonics and partials. There is, however, more to the difference between harmonics and partials than the fact that partials are allowed to be inharmonic.

A partial is one discrete audible ingredient of the piano tone. However, the simplest element or ingredient of audible sound is the *pure tone* (a single pure tone can be generated electronically from a *sine wave*).

A single piano tone partial does not necessarily have to be a pure tone. A partial may contain two or more pure tones, with slightly different frequencies. This is a second, very important feature of piano tone partials, that makes them different to harmonics, and is a feature that can occur in addition to inharmonicity or the effects of string stiffness.[3]

False beats and decay

Returning to the ladder analogy, a partial is represented by a rung on the ladder. If an audible partial of a single piano string does contain two or more pure tones, at slightly different frequencies, the partial itself can sometimes exhibit *beating*, because these pure tones are, so to speak, acting like a double or multiple rung in place of a single rung, on the string's own individual "partial ladder".

The slight misalignment between the double rungs in this position, occurring on the one ladder, causes beating. Beating produced by a single string is referred to by piano tuners as *false* beating. False beats are typically "inherited" in any interval that includes that string, and they cannot have their beat *rate* very successfully altered or "tuned out" by adjusting the tension on the string.

Piano tuners may view "false beats" as a kind of occasional "fault", or an acoustical obstacle to the ideal of "eliminating

---

[3] A fluctuating or beating partial can be regarded as a single frequency with modulated amplitude, or as more than one frequency. There is a mathematical equivalence between the two. "Artificially" modulating the amplitude of a single frequency signal with a regular beat, typically results in triple frequency components.

the beat". In fact, the false beats that are noticed in this way by tuners, are an appearance of a natural part of piano tone that is much more pervasive. Essentially the same phenomenon can be present in many instances where it will not necessarily be labelled as "falseness", but will nonetheless have a significant effect on tone and tuning. The reality is that the difference between what tuners declare "false" or "not false", is only a matter of degree, and the phenomenon itself is a natural and ubiquitous part of the generalised behaviour. To use the ladder analogy again, the design of the ladder naturally allows for multiple rungs to appear at each rung position, rather than necessarily restricting each ladder to only one rung per rung position.

The ladder analogy is limited in that it only represents frequencies. Real partials have important features other than frequency. One of these is *decay*, or the fact that they "die away". "Traditional" theory ignores both falseness and decay, or at best they are each treated as a simple "add on" to the theory. The true nature of piano tone and the way it varies with tuning, actually lies very much in the way falseness and decay interact as a complete system.

New ideas

Although from "traditional" theory we would expect well tuned unisons to have equal frequency fundamentals, Martin and Ward[4] in 1954, noted that expert tuners did not necessarily tune the fundamentals of the unison strings to equal frequencies.

Then in 1959 an experiment by Kirk[5] seemed to indicate that musicians actually preferred the sound of unisons with a small frequency difference between the fundamentals of the strings, to those with no frequency difference. Kirk's results also suggested that piano tuners might be deliberately tuning small frequency differences between the fundamentals of unison group strings.

Other unexpected results appeared in investigations into the decay rates (the rate of "dying away") of piano tones. In 1947 and 1973 Martin, Chase Hundley, and Benioff found that unison partials typically exhibit a dual decay rate in which the first part of the overall decay may have several

[4] Martin, DW, and Ward, WD, 'Subjective Evaluation of Musical Scale Temperament in Pianos' JASA, 26, 1954, 932(A); 33, 1962, pp. 582-585.

[5] Kirk, RE, 'Tuning Preferences for Piano Unison Groups', JASA, 31, 1959, pp. 1644 – 1648,.

times the decay rate of the later part.[6] Benade[7] suggested in 1976 that the decay rate of the unison should initially be three times that of the single string.

He reasoned that when all three strings vibrate in phase, as they do initially, the force exerted on the bridge is three times that of a single string alone, the bridge motion is tripled, and the rate of energy loss is thus tripled. After a little time the strings lose their phase relationship and the decay rate falls to equal that of a single string.

This explanation seemed to lend weight to the notion that frequency discrepancies deliberately tuned between the fundamentals of the individual trichord strings, were an advantage. The strings of a unison "too perfectly tuned", so to speak, would not lose their phase relationship very quickly, so the unison would simply decay too fast.

The argument was that expert tuners introduce "mistunings" between the strings of the trichord in order to improve the decay time – "perfectly tuned" unisons, it was argued, die away too rapidly and sound too dull.

In 1977 Weinreich[8] showed in a seminal paper that the *decay rate* of a partial of a two stringed unison is strongly dependent on the mistuning between the strings when the mistuning is small. Furthermore, at small mistunings, the *beat rate* itself is not as dependent on the mistuning as "traditional" theory supposes.

---

[6] Martin, DW, 'Decay rates of piano tones', *JASA*, 19,4, 1947, pp. 535-541; Chase Hundley, T, Benioff, H, and Martin, DW, 'Factors contributing to the multiple rate of piano tone decay', *JASA*, 64,5, 1973, pp. 1303-1309.

[7] Benade, AH, *Fundamentals of musical acoustics*, NY, 1976, p. 336.

[8] Weinreich, G, 'Coupled piano tones', *JASA*, 62, 6, 1977, pp. 1474-1484.

This is because neither the frequencies nor the decay rates produced by the unison with both strings sounding, are necessarily the same as those produced by the individual strings, sounding alone. Weinreich's mathematical model suggested that in the finest tuning region, piano tuners might be making changes that primarily affect partial decay rates, rather than beat rates. Importantly, zero mistuning between the strings does not necessarily mean a beatless unison, and a small mistuning does not necessarily result in a regular beat rate at all.

The decay rate of a partial would also be affected by the phase relationship between the strings, and Weinreich hypothesised that the latter can be affected by small irregularities in the hammers, causing strings to begin vibrating at different times, or with different amplitudes.

Small mistunings might, Weinreich suggested, be being deliberately introduced by expert tuners as a consequence of altering the decay rates of partials in order to compensate for hammer irregularities. In other words, irregularities in the tones of unisons caused by less than uniform hammer condition, are naturally overcome to some degree by the expert tuner's attention to unison tone in the fine tuning process.

Three essential features arise from these developments, which are now well recognised. Firstly, the decay of a piano unison partial is not necessarily at a constant rate, but may exhibit a *dual decay rate*, the first part of the decay being rapid, and the second part coming after this, being considerably less rapid. The first rapid part of the decay is called the *prompt sound*, and the latter part that dies away much more slowly, is called the *aftersound*.

Secondly, the "traditional" rule for beat rates being equal to the mistuning between two partials, does not necessarily hold for small mistunings. Thirdly, in changing small mistunings between strings, it is not just the beat rates but also the decay rates of partials, and in particular the *aftersound*, that can be altered.

It is not that expert tuners have to think about these concepts consciously in the process of tuning. Rather, we are saying that merely "eliminating the beat" at "zero mistuning" is not what fine tuning as carried out by the artist tuner, is all about.

To see why expert tuners making the finest adjustments to the tuning of the unison, are going well beyond "eliminating beating", and are controlling other factors that alter the tone of the unison in more complex ways, we have to cast out some of the old ideas of "traditional" theory and start afresh with a more contemporary approach. The best way to do this is to begin with the Weinreich model. This is the simplest model recognising that piano strings are *coupled* by the bridge and soundboard.

The Weinreich model for a resistive bridge

The Weinreich model is for two unison strings vibrating in one plane. The strings are side by side on the bridge, so the properties of the bridge are considered to be the same for both strings. The model is concerned with the behaviour of just one partial, which for convenience we shall assume here to be the fundamental of the unison, but the model will apply just as well for any given partial.

The *mistuning* then, is defined as the difference between the fundamental frequencies of the two strings, when each is sounding alone. When both strings are struck together, we are then looking at an oscillating system comprised of two strings plus a moveable bridge boundary. This is a system of two *coupled oscillators*.

Coupled system behaviour can be very complicated to compute, but Weinreich approached the problem with great elegance by "importing" a technique from particle physics. The power of the technique lies in that it does not require absolute parameter values to be known in order to predict behaviour.

The possible range of behaviour is dependent only on relative parameter values (numerous instances of this kind occur in physics, and utilise a technique called *normalisation* in which parameter values range only from 0 to 1 (or 0 to -1, or 0 to i, etc.)).

"Traditional" theory states that the beat rate is equal to the mistuning. In other words, reduce the mistuning to zero, and the beat will vanish. We are interested in the beat rate, but we are now also interested in the relationship between the mistuning and the *decay rate* of the partial. "Traditional" theory only talks about beat rates, and not about decay rates. Piano tuners listen deliberately to beat rates, not decay rates, so why are decay rates so important?

Decay rates are important because they can affect the beat pattern, and can even make it disappear. Fig. (1) shows some graphical representations of what can happen to a theoretical beat pattern when decay is taken into account. The vertical scale represents loudness, and the horizontal scale is time.

Fig. I

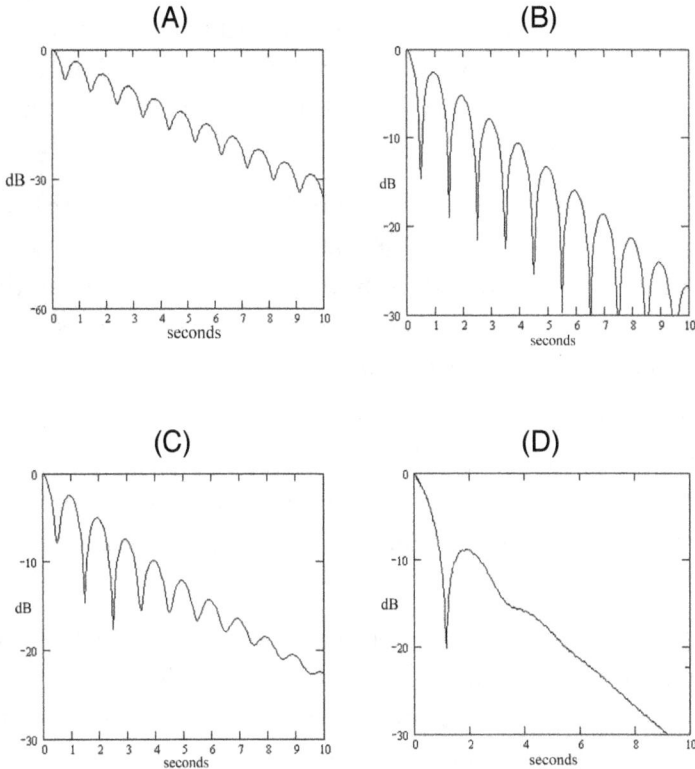

Fig. I. Beat patterns have significant features in addition to *beat rate*. These are *beat amplitude* (the "depth" of the beat), and *beat decay rate*, which is distinct from the overall partial decay rate.

These theoretical partials all *decay*, that is, they get quieter as time goes on. As can be seen from the illustrations, when *decay* is included in the theory, a beat does not just have a beat *rate*, but also has a beat *amplitude* that we must consider, which is the depth of the beat from the top of the beat to the bottom.

For example, (A) and (B) have the same beat *rate* (1 beat per second), but different beat amplitudes. The amplitude of beat (B) is much greater than the amplitude of beat (A). In (C), the beat rate is still the same, but the beat amplitude changes, as time continues.

In fact, it *grows* at first, and then *decays*. In (A) and (B) the beat also decays of course, because the whole partial is decaying. In (A) and (B), however, the beat decays at the same rate as the partial. In (C), the beat decays at a different rate to the partial overall.

First it grows (to about 2.5 seconds), then it decays faster than the overall partial decay rate. In real piano tones beats that decay faster than the overall partial decay rate are common. For small mistunings, they are the norm, rather than the exception.

If a beat decays *much* faster than the overall partial decay rate, the beat may disappear altogether while the partial is still sounding. If the beat rate is also slow enough compared to the beat *decay rate*, a full beat pattern may never become fully established.

The curve at (D) illustrates this. The beat amplitude is almost zero by about 4 seconds, leading to a decay pattern that is only a "single null" (the "valley" at about 1 second) followed by an almost smooth (beatless) decay after the null.

These patterns of decay can be produced simply by adding together two *decaying* partials. The resultant pattern depends on the relative amplitudes of the two partials at the beginning of the decay time, and their relative decay rates. A beat amplitude will be greatest when the two partials responsible for the beat are equal in amplitude.

The two partials may start with different amplitudes, but may also decay at different rates. The beat amplitude reaches its maximum when the two amplitudes reach the same value. In (A) and (B) the partials added together are equal in initial amplitude and decay rate. In (C), one partial starts with greater amplitude than the other, but also decays faster, the two partials reaching equal amplitude at about 2 seconds.

If two partials begin at about the same amplitude but one partial decays away much faster than the other, the beat amplitude will itself decay and the beat may vanish, as in (D). The partial with the slowest decay rate will be the one persisting later in the overall decay, leading to a dual decay rate overall.

These patterns show what can occur if we simply follow the "traditional" approach of adding together two different frequency partials, but include decay in the equations. They show us that we can expect some different behaviour to "traditional" theory's simple idea that the partial just beats, or not, as the case may be.

This is all very well, but we need to know what the frequencies and decay rates are, in relation to the mistuning. Because the soundboard-bridge couples the two strings, this depends on the properties of the bridge, i.e. its resistive and reactive properties.

Weinreich began by investigating what would happen if the bridge constituted a purely resistive boundary, that is, if it drains energy away from the strings, but its reactive, elastic, inertial, frequency changing properties are negligible. The two strings plus the bridge are one system that has its own *normal modes* of vibration.

These are not the standing waves that would occur on the individual strings sounding alone. "Traditional" theory takes the frequencies of the latter (ignoring decay rates) and adds them together to create the beat pattern, ignoring coupling. In the coupled system we must find the normal mode frequencies and their decay rates, from the coupled system itself.

Weinreich used a *dynamical matrix* method first to extract the mode frequencies and decay rates, assuming the bridge coupling between the two strings is purely resistive. The results for the frequencies and decay rates are shown in Fig. (2), where the vertical axes are frequency or decay rate, and the horizontal axis is the mistuning between the strings, ε .

The mistuning ε is in units that are equal to the single string (uncoupled) partial decay rate, and is an angular frequency. This just means the mistuning in Hz between the strings would be ε/π . The model is configured such that the total mistuning between the two strings (one string relative to the other) is 2ε .

In (A) the vertical axis shows the frequencies of the two modes produced by the coupled system (these are not same as the frequencies of the two separate strings, sounding in isolation). In (B) the vertical axis shows the decay rates of these two modes. The resultant motion of the bridge would be a *superposition* of the two modes, and this would be the motion driving the soundboard and hence the radiated sound.

From (A) it can be seen that as mistuning is reduced, the difference between the two frequencies responsible for the beat reduces rapidly as the total mistuning approaches 2ε. What this mistuning is in Hz, will depend on the single string (uncoupled) partial decay rate. In the mid-compass it will be around 0.3 Hz, but moving up the compass it will get much larger. In the bass, where the decay rates are much smaller (the decay time is much longer), this critical mistuning will be much smaller.

The beat rate created by the superposition of these two frequencies (which will be equal to their difference) will thus dramatically reduce as the mistuning approaches $+\varepsilon$ or $-\varepsilon$, i.e. as the total mistuning approaches 2ε.

At any mistuning less than this, the difference vanishes (there is only one line on the graph in this region) and therefore so does the beat. In other words, in the mid-compass the beat would start to vanish altogether as soon as it was slowed to around 1 beat every three seconds. The string tension could be changed inside this mistuning by an amount, equivalent in "traditional" theory, to passing from 0.3 Hz flat to 0.3 Hz sharp, without introducing a beat.

At the same time, looking at (B), within this same mistuning region, two different decay rates appear. At zero mistuning one decay rate is zero, and the other is twice the single string (uncoupled) partial decay rate.

This means that not only would the beat have disappeared at zero mistuning, but the partial would initially show a *prompt sound* decaying at twice the single string rate, followed by an aftersound that does not decay at all. Within the region at other mistuning values, it is the *decay rates* of the *prompt sound* and *aftersound* that are affected by mistuning changes, rather than any beat rate.

Fig. 2

A

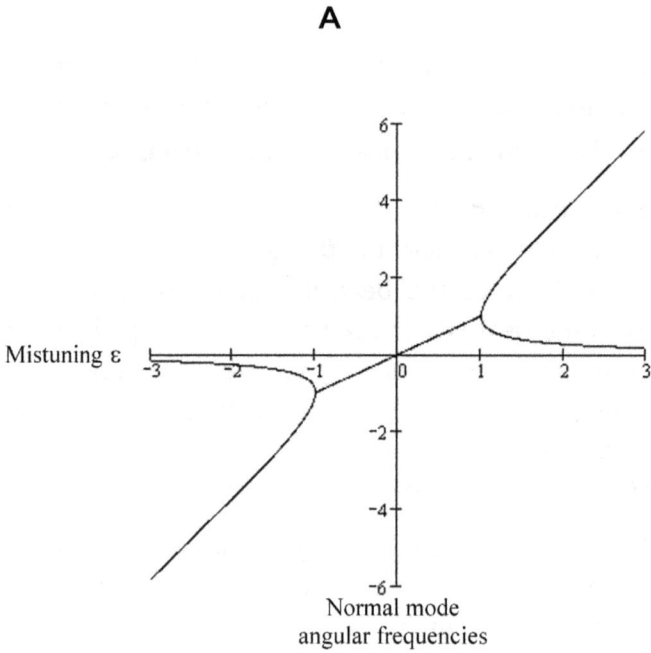

Mistuning ε

Normal mode
angular frequencies

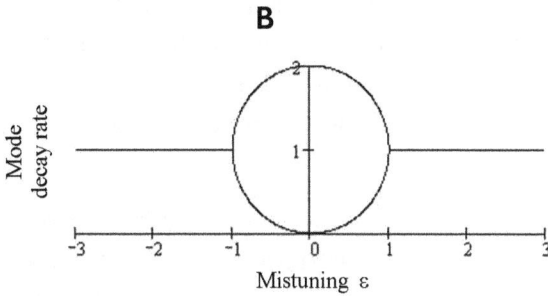

B

Mode decay rate (vertical axis) vs Mistuning ε (horizontal axis)

Fig. 2.

The results of the Weinreich model for two coupled piano unison strings (at one partial), for a (hypothetical) purely resistive bridge, showing how frequencies (A) and decay rates (B) vary with mistuning between the strings. Within a mistuning range equal to twice the single string partial decay rate, the frequencies coalesce so the beat vanishes, whilst two different decay rates appear, causing a faster decaying prompt sound, and slower decaying aftersound. Whilst particularly elegant, it should be remembered that that this *does not apply to real piano strings* which are on a bridge that is both resistive *and* reactive.

A misleading ideal?

This configuration shows one extreme of possible behaviour – the behaviour if the soundboard bridge were (hypothetically) purely resistive and there were no other complicating factors.

A "popularised", simplified version of the theory appeared in *Scientific American* describing the coupled motions of piano strings largely in terms of this hypothetical model. Whilst valid as a simplified model, this may also have allowed the propagation of some popular misconceptions about piano tuning.

The description ties in well with Benade's hypothesis for prompt sound and aftersound in trichords, but both models are over-simplified, compared to the real situation. It should be remembered that the piano bridge is not purely resistive, and that strings do move in two planes, both facts being adequately pointed out by Weinreich in the original paper published in *JASA*.

Perhaps most important of all, the physics of single partial coupling does not in itself "explain" what expert piano tuners are doing in tuning the unison as a whole, because in tuning the unison one does not listen merely to one partial, especially not just the fundamental.

Good unison tuning requires listening to the *whole soundscape* which contains many partials, whose relationships are not always fixed in a rigidly predictable way. In practice, the master tuner listens to *tone*, which is the psycho-acoustic result of all the partials, and how they are behaving as one complex system.

The Weinreich model for a reactive bridge

At the other extreme would be the hypothetical behaviour if the bridge were purely reactive (if it were, the soundboard would not work as an amplifier). Fig. (3) shows the two frequencies produced by the mistuning for the hypothetical purely reactive bridge.

The dotted lines show the two frequencies as they would be according to "traditional" theory. In this case the frequencies produced by the coupled system are further apart than they would be in "traditional" theory. Even at zero mistuning, their difference cannot be eliminated, and a beat would remain. The unison partial would be impossible to tune beatless.

Fig. 3

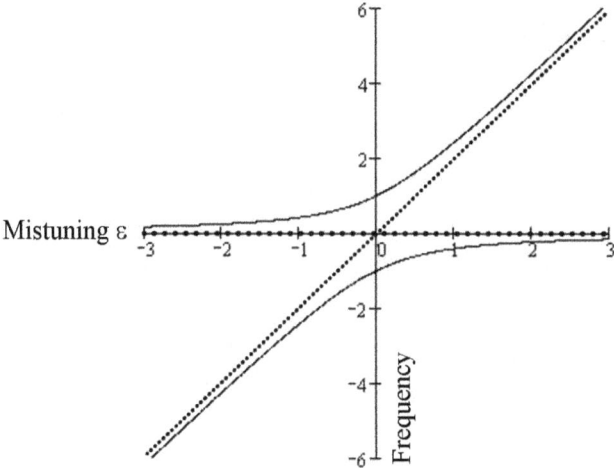

Fig. 3. Results of the Weinreich model for a hypothetical, purely reactive bridge. The difference between the two frequencies cannot be eliminated even at zero mistuning, so a beat would always remain. The dotted lines represent the behaviour as in the "traditional" theory.

The Weinreich model for a "realistic" bridge

As might be expected, in the case of the real piano bridge, the behaviour is somewhere between these two extremes. Fig. (4) shows the results for different bridges with both resistive and reactive components. The different lines are for different component proportions. As might be guessed, the solid lines in (A) which are closest to the shape for the hypothetical purely resistive bridge, are for the bridge with the greatest resistive component. The decay rates for the purely resistive bridge are still shown.

Fig. 4

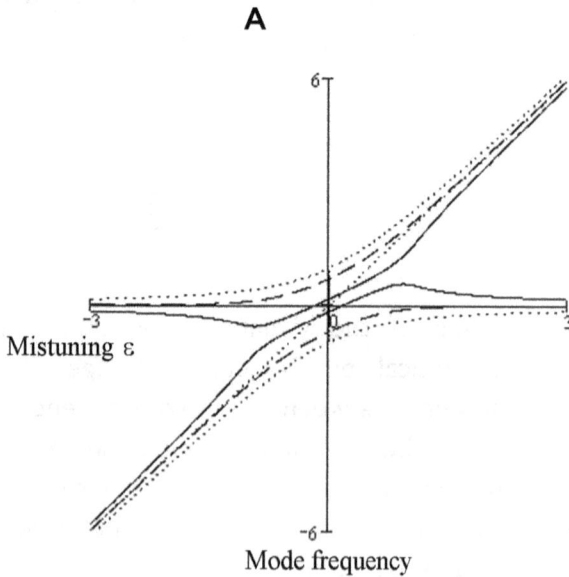

A

Mistuning ε

Mode frequency

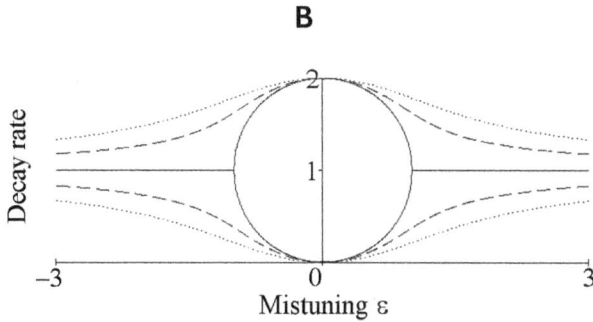

B

Fig. 4. Results of the Weinreich model when the bridge has both resistive and reactive components. The different line types are for different proportions of reactive and resistive component in the bridge coupling.

The solid line is for the most resistive and least reactive. In (B) the solid line is for a purely resistive bridge. The diagonal dotted line through the origin at (A) is the frequency for "traditional" theory. The actual frequency lines *do not cross* at zero mistuning – a frequency difference always remains. However, the decay rates do diverge as the mistuning approaches zero.

The effect on beat patterns

It has sometimes been said that piano unison strings "mode lock". This can give the impression, like Fig. (2), that two strings will "jump into" a "beatless" state as soon as the mistuning between them is reduced to certain value. It must be stressed that this is not the general case, either in practice or in theory.

41

It is important to note that in the Weinreich model applied to a real piano bridge which is both resistive *and* reactive, the two frequencies *do not* coalesce or "lock together". In fact, close to or at zero mistuning the two frequencies are actually *further apart* than they would be in "traditional" theory.

However, in practice, at small mistunings we *can* eliminate the beat in a given partial, and often rather easily, even though a frequency difference remains. The theory does in fact express this, but not through "mode locking". The reason lies in the decay rates, not in the frequencies entirely "coalescing" or "locking together". Within the "critical tuning range", the decay rates diverge, *but also* the beat rate is relatively slow, because the frequency difference is small.

We are then in the situation already described at Fig. (1D). In effect, the beat "decays faster than it can beat". It is the difference in decay rates that finally "kills off" the beat, not the equalising of the component frequencies. Thus, generalised statements that coupled piano unison strings "mode lock" are not correct. Nevertheless, there is still a *range* of mistunings, rather than a single one of zero, over which the beat may disappear or be replaced with a single null.

Fig. (5) shows the kind of decay patterns that can occur with resistive and reactive bridge coupling, for various bridge configurations, when the mistuning is small. These are decay curves generated from the Weinreich matrix, and show how the decay pattern or "beat", changes as mistuning is reduced. At (A) and (B) the mistuning decreases from solid to dashed to dotted lines.

At (C) mistuning decreases from dashed to solid to dotted lines, and at (D) mistuning decreases from dotted to dashed to solid lines. In all cases, as the mistuning is reduced, the beat not only slows down (the beat length gets longer), but its own decay rate increases, which contributes also to the "elimination" of the beat. The closer the mistuning is to zero, the slower the decay rate of the aftersound, after the last beat, or after the single null.

Fig. 5

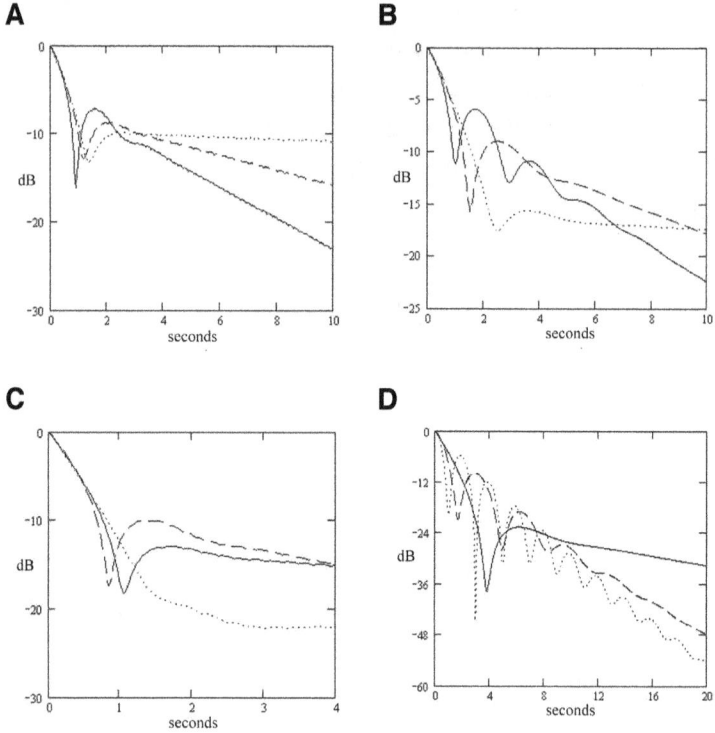

Fig. 5.

Four different sets of partials (A, B, C and D), each of 3 example decay curves generated from the matrix theory for a "realistic" bridge. In each case, as the mistuning is reduced, the beat length gets longer (the beat rate decreases) and the rate at which the beat itself decays (as distinct from the overall partial) increases, eventually causing the beat to disappear after an initial single null. Also, as mistuning is reduced, the aftersound (the part after the null) decay rate decreases.

Note that once the beat starts to vanish (or turn into a single null) the different mistunings (dotted, dashed and solid lines) control the *decay rate of the aftersound* rather than the beat rate.

Although the Weinreich model is itself still a simplified model of the real situation, it illustrates the importance of decay mechanisms in beat formation, and that at smaller mistunings, the regular beat pattern of "traditional" theory (which itself is simplified) is not necessarily to be expected.

Perhaps the most important consequence of decaying slow beats, as far as beat rates are concerned, is that a regular beat may sometimes be eliminated *before* the mistuning is zero, and may typically be replaced by a single null after which the decay is more or less "beatless", depending on the parameters. It is then the aftersound decay rate that is being adjusted by further changes to the mistuning.

Practical consequences - beat attenuation

The primary outcome of taking decay rates into account as well as beat rates, is that the "elimination" of beats is found to be achieved not only by reducing the beat *rate*. Beats may in general be *attenuated* by reducing the beat *amplitude*, or increasing the beat decay rate. This profoundly increases the tone control possibilities available to the tuner, over those that the "traditional" theory suggests.

A beat can indeed disappear because the beat rate becomes sufficiently slow, in comparison to the overall decay time. However, a beat can also disappear because its amplitude vanishes, or is too small to allow the beat to be detected.

Both the beat rate and the amplitude decay rate, are in general affected by the mistuning, at small mistuning values. At small mistuning values, it is generally the aftersound decay rate that is most affected by mistuning changes, rather than the apparent beat rate.

The trichord in two planes

Piano tuners do not, of course, tune unisons by listening to just one partial. There are many partials in the unison, and they will all beat with their own beat rates, or behave in their own "coupled" way, at a sufficiently small mistunings. Changes to many partials happen simultaneously.

All the partials together contribute to the tone of the unison, which for expert tuners is what matters. Nevertheless, from a theoretical point of view, before understanding what happens in the spectrum as a whole, it is still enlightening to understand how each partial might behave, so it is useful to extend the Weinreich model for the behaviour of a single partial.

It is possible to extend the Weinreich model to include all three strings of the trichord, and to include string motion in two planes. The theoretical results then generated are *much* more complicated, but broadly similar theoretical decay curve behaviour can be observed at small mistunings.

The behaviour appears to indicate that the largest mistuning between strings in a trichord can be approximately twice as large as in the unison pair, at the point where a regular beat is reduced to a single null. This would place the "preferred mistunings" in trichords found by Kirk, well inside this range.

Chaotic trichords?

The extended dynamical matrix model for the full trichord with two transverse degrees of freedom (vibrations in two planes) is not only much more complicated, but appears in computer generated results to be capable of *bifurcation behaviour* (splitting of values in a graph) in the frequencies and decay rates, when a reactive bridge component is present.

This has not been fully investigated, but if this is not a computing artefact, the trichord in two planes could be especially interesting. This would not be because it is neatly solvable, but because bifurcation behaviour is normally indicative of chaotic, complex dynamics.

In other words, the full trichord may even be a complex, chaotic system (the weather is a "classic" example of a complex, chaotic system). This would make the precise behaviour of a given trichord difficult or impossible to predict in advance.

Beyond the Weinreich model – falseness

The resistive and reactive parts of the bridge's properties collectively constitute what is known as the bridge *admittance* (or its inverse, the *impedance*). Motion in two planes becomes important when the bridge admittance is *anisotropic*, meaning it is not equal in all transverse directions.

The soundboard is designed as an elastic structure with a "crown" (or "buck"). This means the soundboard surface is designed as a shallow, two-dimensional arch, assisted by the curvature on the belly bars. The arching resists the collective downbearing force from the strings.

Weinreich found on a grand piano that despite this structural design feature, the reactive (frequency changing) part of the bridge admittance is *approximately* equal in all transverse directions. The resistive (decay causing) part is, as might be expected, much greater in the vertical direction.

The question arises, what is the effect when the reactive bridge admittance is not exactly equal in all transverse directions? So far we have seen the Weinreich model shows that at small mistunings the decay rate is very dependent on the mistuning, and becomes important in the formation of beats and decay patterns.

As a result of this, mistunings may naturally occur between the strings of a unison tuned by an expert tuner, where the tuner is not only "eliminating the beat" but also adjusting, in particular, the *aftersound* part of the decay. Further theory shows, however, that a small directional inequality, or *anisotropy* in the reactive part of the bridge admittance, is capable of producing much more complicated motion than the Weinreich model itself describes.

When anisotropy in the bridge admittance is taken into account, the theory then shows that if the tuner is attempting simply to reduce or eliminate beating, mistunings may occur between the strings simply because the minimum beating or fluctuation in the decay curve does not necessarily occur at zero mistuning.[9]

---

[9] Capleton, B, *False beats in coupled piano string unisons, JASA*, 115 (2), 2004, 885-892.

The effect of anisotropy in the reactive part of the bridge admittance can result in what tuners know as *false beats* (already mentioned above), which are beats that occur in partials of the single string sounding alone. False beats occurring in a partial of a single, isolated string of a unison pair, are in general inherited in some form by the equivalent partial of the unison.

The controlling of these inherited false beats in the unison, by changing the string tension, follows very different rules of behaviour to the controlling of the normal adjustable beats where no falseness is present. In general - and unlike normal beat rates that arise where no falseness is present - the beat rate of an inherited false beat is relatively insensitive to changes of string tension over the whole fine tuning range. However, this does not mean that the beating in the unison will be entirely unadjustable.

Usually, at small mistunings, the beat *amplitude* becomes sensitive to changes of mistuning, and even the beat *rate* can be affected in a limited way. The beat can therefore be attenuated through changes in mistuning, to a limited extent by changing its beat rate, and to a greater extent by reducing its amplitude. The beat can also be attenuated by increasing the decay rate of the partial, so that the beating partial is eliminated from the overall tone recipe as soon as possible.

Sometimes, the amplitude of fluctuations in a partial where falseness is present, can be most reduced at zero mistuning, but other times, a small mistuning may give the best result. What mistuning might be required where, is a very complicated issue.

The theoretical result depends on the sixteen parameters for a unison pair described by the dynamical matrix model for a unison pair in two planes. The practical results will depend on the "severity" of the falseness and the skill and artistry of the tuner.

The idea of reducing the effects of false beats by introducing mistunings was in principle recognised by Braid White in 1917,[10] when he suggested false beats could be "neutralized" by tuning the strings "slightly off".

It is important to appreciate that this is not a question of merely "masking" false beat phenomena with additional movement in the unison decay pattern. The decay pattern itself is improved by actually reducing the amplitude of false beat fluctuations.

---

[10] Braid White, W, *Piano Tuning and Allied Arts*, 1917, 14th reprint 1972, p. 106.

Observing real piano strings

The kind of behaviour described by dynamical matrix theory can often be observed in the decay envelopes of the actual audible sound radiated by the soundboard (the sound we hear from the piano, and to which piano tuners listen).

These visual representations of real partial decay patterns can be readily generated through digital analysis, and usually represent energy rather than loudness on the vertical axis. The theoretical graphs we have been looking at so far show decibels rather than energy on the vertical axis.

This is a logarithmic scale with zero and negative values only, a scale system that represents the normal "smooth" decay as a straight line. A perfectly "smooth", natural decay is actually exponential, and without the use of a logarithmic scale it appears as an exponential curve.

Fig. (5) shows, for comparison, a number of different types of decay pattern examples in both the logarithmic and sound envelope representations (from actual piano tones). From top to bottom, they represent the kind of progressive change in decay pattern that could be expected as one attempts to reduce the beat rate in a single partial of a unison pair, where reactive and dissipative (resistive component) bridge coupling is present.

Fig. 5

Theoretical logarithmic representation

Regular beat, decaying at the same rate as the partial

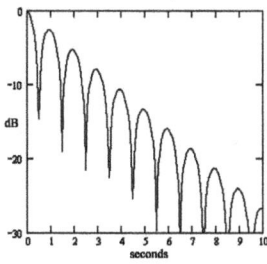

Actual envelope representation

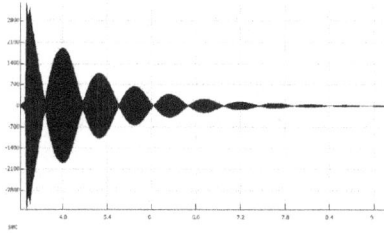

Regular beat, decaying faster than the partial

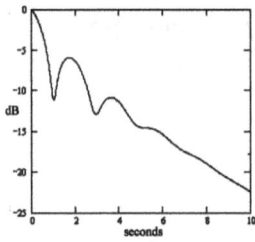

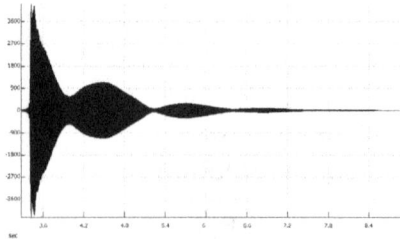

Single null and beat

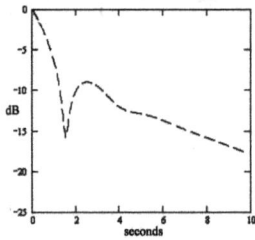

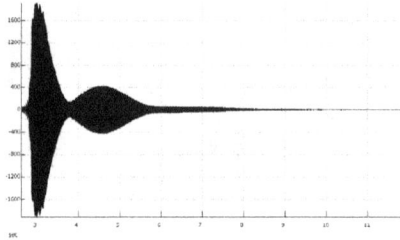

Single null

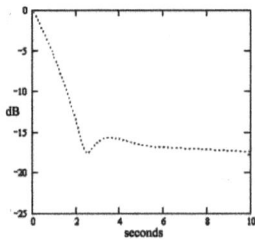

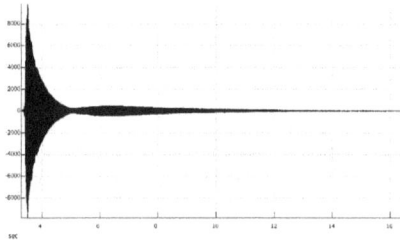

"Beatless" decay

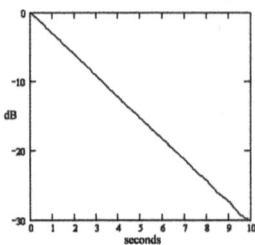

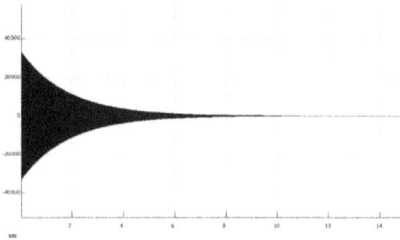

The "beatless" decay illustrated above is a straightforward exponential decay, with only one decay rate. An audibly "beatless" decay can also occur where there is a dual decay rate. Fig (6) shows an example.

Fig. 6

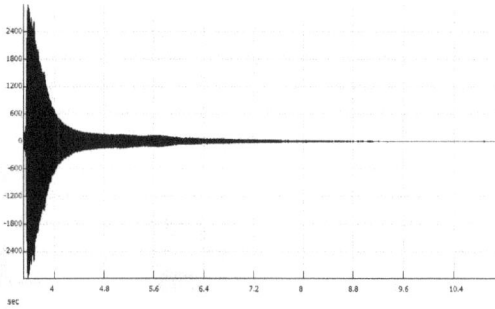

In the examples Fig. (5), as the mistuning is reduced from top to bottom, the beat rate never really gets any slower than about one beat in two seconds, but rather, begins to convert at this beat rate to a single null, and then to a smooth exponential decay.

This pattern of behaviour in piano unison partials is common – as the beat rate slows, the beat decay rate increases. As mistuning is reduced, there is not simply a regular beat with reducing beat rate. Rather, as mistuning is reduced, a regular beat converts to a single beat, then to a single null, then to a beatless decay.

A false unison pair

Fig. (7) shows the decay envelopes of the second partial of two individual unison strings, each sounding alone, and of the two strings sounding together as a unison pair. The strings are the left and middle strings of the note A49 on a Steinway model M.

Fig. 7

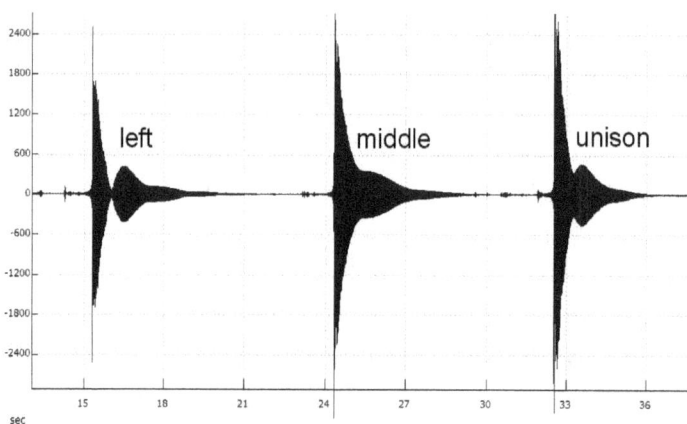

The left string is false on its second partial (the fundamentals of both strings are not false), the false beat rate being around I per second. The beat is clearly visible in the decay envelope, and is "prominent" because the beat amplitude is large – the initial null is very deep.

The middle string is also slightly false on its second partial, but much less prominently (the null has very little depth). The unison (tuned to a subjectively judged "optimum" tone condition) inherits a beat in its second partial, but one that is much less prominent the false string alone – the depth of the null and hence the amplitude of the beat is reduced, compared to the single left string.

A similar situation is found at the third partial, Fig. (8), where the unison's partial is "better" than those of the individual strings, the beat having been attenuated here also.

Fig. 8

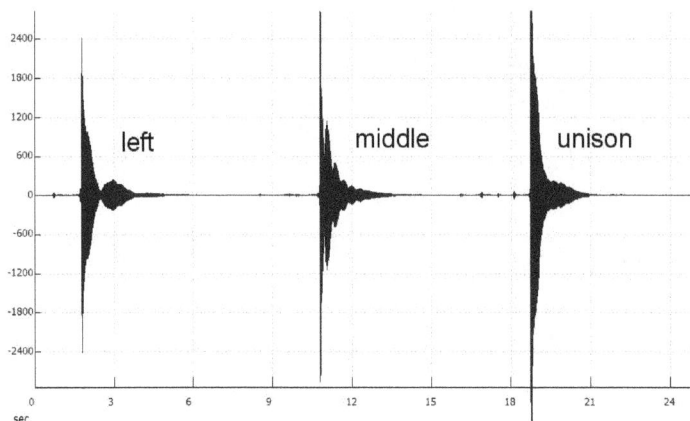

The mechanism of "hiding" falseness

The "improvement" on the false beating left string is not due to the fact that false beating is "masked" by additional beating in the unison. Rather, the false beat patterns are each individually attenuated. An "improvement" effect occurs in the strong partials shown, and also in the other (weaker) partials also, up to the 8th partial (higher partials were not analysed).

Analysis often shows that where faster false beating in higher partials has not been "eliminated", it has nevertheless been attenuated by increasing the overall decay rate. An example is shown in Fig. (9), of the 6th partial of the unison.

Fig. 9

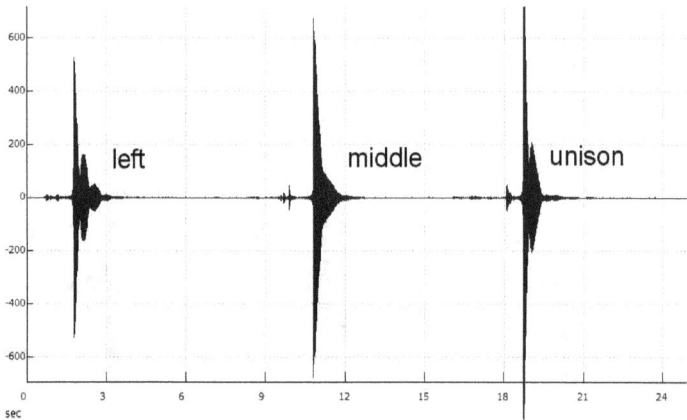

Falseness in a Steinway unison pair A37

An analysis of the middle and right strings of the unison A37 on the same Steinway model M, together with the two strings sounding as a unison pair, shows some of the features of unison tuning that go well beyond the idea that one should simply "tune out the beat".

The analysis clearly shows false beat patterns (both visually, and aurally in the digitally isolated partials) occurring in the middle string, on 10 of the 22 partials, and on the right string in 9 partials. At first sight this seems surprising, and sounds as though we are describing a very poor instrument, rather than a Steinway! In fact, no noticeable "problem" due to falseness presents itself on hearing and tuning these strings – the "falseness" goes more or less unnoticed in normal tuning practice.

This is because it is neither sufficiently prominent (as beat amplitude) nor sufficiently fast-beating for the string to properly qualify as a "false string" in the "ordinary language" of piano tuners. Once the digitally filtered, isolated partials are heard, however, they are then relatively easy to distinguish as false in the overall tone.

Whilst some strings may perhaps show no false beat patterns up to the 22nd partial, the fact is that strings on even the best instruments may also readily exhibit this behaviour. The cause, at the very least, can be just because the general physical configuration for the system of piano strings *in situ*, allows for parametric transverse motion in two planes.

That musical instrument strings struck or plucked in one plane start vibrating in the perpendicular plane, is well known in musical acoustics. Such behaviour cannot take place unless there are non-degenerate normal modes of the system not in line with the initial motion.

Close-frequency normal mode pairs can be formed where the reactive part of the bridge admittance is not the same in all transverse directions. At middle C there would need to be a variation in the order of 6:1 to produce a 1 Hz beat in the fundamental, and this is not normally encountered.

However, where the reactive bridge admittance is smaller and the frequency is higher, e.g. for notes higher in the compass or for higher partials, the theory shows that smaller ratios can produce faster beats.[11]

There is no particular reason why we should expect perfect bridge isotropy at every partial frequency, and hence no reason to expect beat patterns from this cause to be entirely absent. Furthermore, an anisotropic bridge-boundary may not be the only cause of beating in single string partials.

Whether or not a physical beat in the motion of the string actually manifests from bridge anisotropy, will depend on the relationship between the decay rates, and the geometrical configuration of the system's normal modes.

The audible beat is then further affected by how the soundboard radiates the sound. In any event, the "natural behaviour" is one that allows for beat patterns in partials of a single string, rather than one that necessarily excludes them.

Piano tuners, however, may in many cases tend to remark on a string being "false" only when this natural phenomenon is particular "severe", and presents difficulties to the ideal of "tuning out the beat". The relationship between beat patterns in single string partials and instrument quality, is an interesting one that merits further research.

Most tuners would be aware that very poor quality instruments suffer from widespread, severe falseness over the compass. However, whilst it is a characteristic of some

---

[11] Capleton, *op. cit.*

60

high quality instruments that the strings are very "pure" (the piano tuning term for the opposite of falseness), other instruments of quality can nevertheless still exhibit a relatively high incidence of falseness.

One of the shortcomings of the "tuning out the beat" edict of "traditional" theory is that false beat phenomena can consequently be denigrated as a "fault", when in fact they are a natural feature of piano tone behaviour, that only warrants being labelled as a "fault" when they reach a certain magnitude or become excessive in practical terms.

Given that false beat phenomena are adjusted more through amplitude and decay rate, than through beat rate, it is more realistic to refer to this aspect of unison tuning in terms of *reducing movement* in the soundscape. This still applies in (possibly only hypothetical) cases where all movement is stopped.

There is in any case no single "beat" in all unisons that must be "tuned out" with priority over all others. The soundscape is a tone recipe of ingredient partials, all of which count in the overall recipe. The "ideal" aim may be to eliminate movement as far as possible, but in a situation where some movement must remain, the question *what* movement *where* in the spectrum, can be complex.

Movement can in any case occur simply because the initial amplitudes and decay rates of partials differ, so that the proportions of ingredients in the tone recipe constantly changes. The ability to change decay rates through mistuning becomes, in this respect, another aspect of adjusting movement in the soundscape, distinct from adjusting true beat rates.

Behaviour of the unison in fine tuning

The unison pair A37 of the Steinway M was tuned in six different stages, the first tuning being considered an "optimum" aural tuning. After this, over the next four stages the unison was progressively "spoilt", with no other criteria being applied. An additional last tuning was one in which the second partial specifically, was tuned so that fluctuation in this one partial was reduced to the minimum the unison allowed in practice. The reason for this will be discussed below.

Although the tuning stages are conveniently labelled as "optimum" and "spoilt", the analysis does not investigate what may constitute good or poor tuning. Rather, it shows how the unison behaves in relation to fine tuning variations, and how the complexity of this behaviour allows variations beyond the concept of "tuning out the beat".

The analysis shows at the "optimum" tuning the same general principles discussed above, with respect to "hiding falseness", at work up to the 22nd partial (higher partials were not examined). Both the stage 1 "optimum" tuning and the stage 2 tuning in which the "optimum" was considered slightly spoilt, share some important features.

Up to the 22nd partial, at both the stage 1 "optimum" aural tuning, and the stage 2 tuning, some beat patterns persist in the unison, and these are clearly related to beat or single null patterns found at corresponding partials in the single strings.

In other words, in both the optimum and stage 2 tunings, beat or beat-like patterns in the unison partials occur where false beat patterns also exist at that partial number in one or both of the single strings. However, at *both* these tuning stages *no* beat patterns in the unison occur where the corresponding partials in the single strings are themselves free of false beats, or other decay patterns such as the single null.[12]

Small differences in the decay patterns between one tuning and the other do exist, where beat patterns occur. In particular, the highest of the partials have slightly slower beat rates or greater decay rates in the "optimum" tuning.

Data results

The analysis of the unison pair of up to the 22nd partial, generates 110 decay envelopes – five aurally distinguishable stages of tuning each analysed into 22 partials.

In referring to frequency values of a radiated partial found by digital analysis (FFT), it must borne in mind that the natural frequency may not be constant in all cases. Furthermore, FFT precision is limited by the ratio of the sampling frequency to the signal length. The FFT precision in the case in question limits the accuracy of the mistuning measured between the fundamentals of the strings to a

---

[12] All cases in digital analysis of the tone are generally potentially subject to "edge effects", which are rapid fluctuations along the envelope edge. These can be caused by noise, or may be caused by weak interference from other sources, including other piano strings. These fluctuations are generally inaudible compared to false beats. On the latter, see, for example, *Beating frequency and amplitude modulation of the piano tone due to coupling of tones*, Cartling, Bo, JASA, April 2005, 117, 4, pp. 2259-2267.

tolerance of ± 0.023 Hz. The progression of mistunings then becomes:

Tuning stage	Mistuning at the fundamental
1 ("optimum")	0 ± 0.023 Hz
2	- 0.023 ± 0.023 Hz
3	- 0.138 ± 0.023 Hz
4	- 0.137 ± 0.023 Hz
5	- 0.366 ± 0.023 Hz

The minus indicates that the right hand string was progressively *lowered* in tension. The fundamental frequency of the "untuned" middle string changes by 0.115 Hz over the five stages as:

Tuning stage	Fundamental frequency
1 ("optimum")	219.315 ± 0.0115 Hz
2	219.292 ± 0.0115 Hz
3	219.269 ± 0.0115 Hz
4	219.177 ± 0.0115 Hz
5	219.200 ± 0.0115 Hz

The data obtained using "standard" equipment precludes mathematical functional relationships from the matrix theory being confirmed or otherwise, but nevertheless allows other important observations to be made. Firstly, there is the question of tuning precision.

The smallest change in mistuning could (statistically) have been infinitesimal, but the *largest* possible changes between adjacent stages 3 and 4, and between stages 1 and 2, are 0.047 Hz and 0.069 Hz, respectively. This corresponds to a change of 0.37 cents and 0.55 cents, respectively.

Between the "optimum" tuning and stage 3, the mistuning change is at most 0.184 Hz and at least 0.092 Hz. Stage 3 is the first stage at which beats are introduced into partials that were "beatless" in stages 1 and 2, i.e. in partials whose counterparts in the single strings show no false beats. This applies to all analysed partials.

This means the mistuning introduced at the stage where otherwise "avoidable" beats start to become present, is somewhere between 0.727 cents and 1.452 cents (mean value 1.089 cents). This is comparable with the results found by Kirk, that the maximum mistuning between unison strings preferred by musically trained subjects was around 1 cent, and the maximum preferred by all subjects tested was 1 – 2 cents. (Kirk was, however, testing trichords rather than unison pairs). By stages 4 and 5 beating is exhibited in every partial.

The results of this particular unison allow for the possibility that the aurally "optimum" tuning (as judged by the tuner) occurs at zero mistuning. The visual differences between stages 1 and 2 in this unison indicate that at least in part, what was being done in the tuning process, was the "improvement" of decay patterns associated with false beat inheritance, particularly in the higher partials.

The case of the 2nd partial

Fig. (10) shows the progression of decay curves for the first three partials of the unison over the five tuning stages. The 3rd partial passes from "beatless" to beating from stage 2 to stage 3. (These are not all to the same scale, but show the presence of repeated beats, single nulls or "beatless" decays).

The fundamental passes from a "beatless" decay at stages 1 and 2 to single null and then a beat, at stages 3 to 5. The second partial, however, retains a slow repeating beat of approximately the same form over stages 1 to 4, despite the mistuning being changed. The retention of a beat form despite such changes in mistuning, is indicative of false beat inheritance.

The 2nd partials of the single strings, however, exhibit only single nulls, rather than a repeating beat pattern. The general rule for inherited false beats in a single partial is that the beat form in the unison can be "improved" over the form in the single string partial. The reason for the unison's 2nd partial being in this case "worse" than the 2nd partials of the single strings, is discussed below.

Fig. 10

Stage	Partial 1	Partial 2	Partial 3
1	0	0.25	0
2	0	0.25 - 0.5	0
3	5N	0.25 - 0.5	0.5
4	5N	0.25 - 0.05	1
5	0.4	0.75	1.25

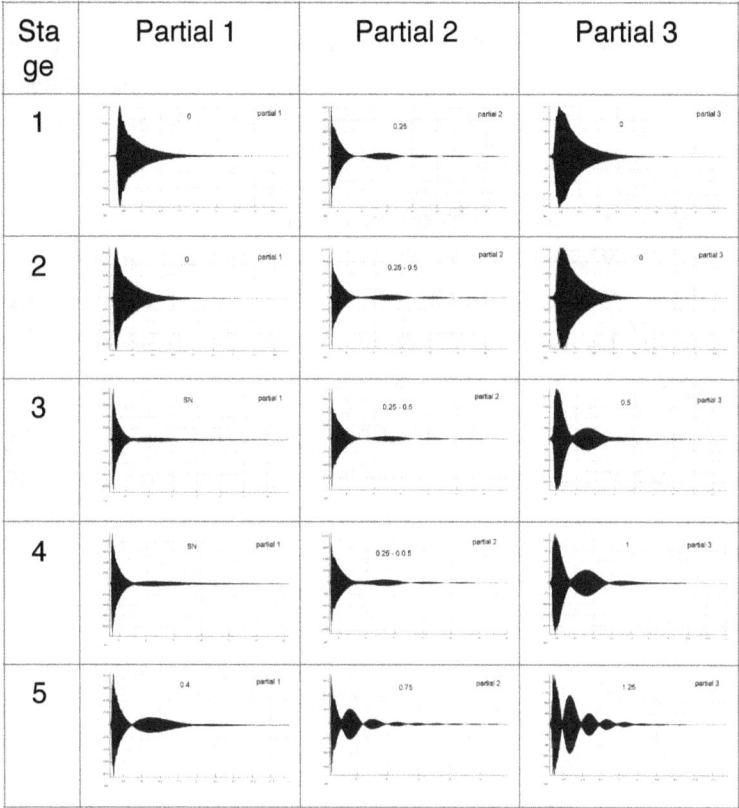

False beat inheritance in the 2nd partial

The inheritance mechanism for false beats is not necessarily straightforward. A false beat in a single string partial indicates that a close-frequency pair of components is generated by the single string and its bridge-boundary. In general, where this is the case, a close-frequency pair will also be generated by the unison at the same partial number.

Piano tuners often experience this in practice as the single string false beat appearing to be present in the sound of the unison. If frequency analysis shows a double or multiple frequency peak in the spectrum of the single string, a double or multiple peak will also generally occur in the same frequency region of the unison spectrum.

However, the precise frequencies and decay rates need not necessarily be the same as those in the single string case, and generally are not. The precise form of the audible false beat in the unison would not therefore, necessarily be expected to be the same as that in the single string.

In the case of the 2nd partial here, both of the single string decays exhibit single null behaviour, rather than a complete beat pattern, Fig. (11).

Fig. 11

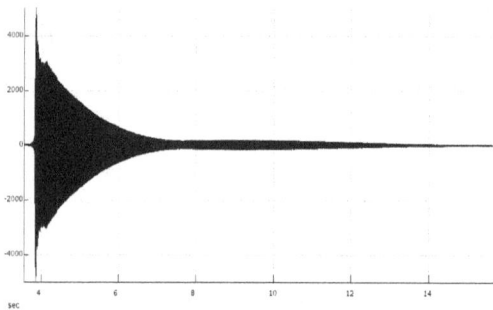

Fig. 11. The (shallow) single null decay of
the middle string's 2nd partial.

This suggests that as far as the 2nd partial of the unison is concerned, the amount of movement in the partial is not optimally reduced at any of the first five stages of tuning. In fact, by tuning the 2nd unison partial specifically, it *is* possible to eliminate regular beating in it, and to reduce the movement to a single null (as already present in the single strings).

The mistuning necessary to achieve this, however, lies *between* the mistunings at stages 2 and 3, and is one at which beats still remain in all the other partials that otherwise be "beatless" at stages 1 and 2. (The "beat" that remains in the fundamental is, however, a single null). The mistuning at this point is 0.092 ± 0.023 Hz.

Summary

The mistuning at the fundamental in this particular unison pair could be zero.

1. A change in mistunings at the fundamental as small as around 0.37 cents results in an audible decrement in soundscape quality (as perceived by the tuner), and a visually changed partial decay set. This result does not preclude the possibility that still smaller changes in mistuning may also have resulted in detectable decrement in soundscape quality. The visible difference between the "optimum" tuning and a "spoilt" tuning with around 0.37 cents extra mistuning, is that some (higher) partials have faster decay rates or slower beat rates, at the "optimum" tuning. These are partials

corresponding to ones that display beat rates in the single strings, i.e. they are "false".

2. In increasing the mistuning at the fundamental, from the "optimum tuning", it is possible that up to around 0.55 cents extra mistuning does not introduce beating into any partials that were not beating to begin with. The decrement in soundscape quality (as perceived by the tuner and seen in the visual decay set) nevertheless occurs over this range.

3. A change in mistunings at the fundamental between 0.727 cents and 1.452 cents does introduce beat patterns in all partials where there was no beat patterns to begin with.

4. The 2nd partials in the single strings exhibit a single null decay (they are false). An "optimum" mistuning exists for the 2nd partial of the unison, in which it just inherits the single null decay pattern, rather than producing a repeating beat. This does not coincide with the mistuning for the "optimum" tuning of the unison as a whole (in which all partials whose counterparts in the single strings are "beatless", are also beatless in the unison).

Some insight into what takes place as the unison is fine tuned can be gleaned by considering the first 4 results in reverse order. The situation represented is then one in which the right hand string would be being raised in tension towards the "target" tuning.

Firstly, as tuning begins, from (4), beat patterns that are not inherited false beats, are removed from the unison partials.

This process might be completed when mistuning at the fundamental is around 0.5 Hz greater than it will be at the "optimum" tuning. The change in mistuning at the fundamental from this point to the "optimum" tuning, then consists mainly of alterations to decay rates and beat amplitudes of partials whose counterparts in the single strings are "false".

The second partial *passes through* its "optimum beatless" condition *before* the "optimum" tuning for the unison is reached, with the result that at the "optimum" tuning for the unison, the 2nd partial actually beats. At the point the 2nd partial is at its "optimum beatless" condition (a single null decay), the unison soundscape contains beating in all measured partials.

The fine tuning process

The general idea that in fine tuning the unison beating is, roughly speaking, eliminated as far as possible, is objectively supported by the results. However, much more than this takes place, and the situation is more complicated. "Elimination" of beating, as far as is possible, may have already taken place by the time the mistuning is reduced to around 0.55 Hz, rather than at zero mistuning, with the single exception of the 2nd partial.

Further changes to the unison soundscape beyond this point are much more complicated than simply being beat elimination. At the "optimum" tuning a beat of around 0.25 Hz remains in the 2nd partial, which in this unison is very strong. Both its high amplitude and small decay rate results in the 2nd partial entirely dominating the tone after about 4 seconds of decay time.

The mistuning could be altered to convert this regular beat into a single null, but this simultaneously introduces a single null into the fundamental, and beat patterns into all other partials that would otherwise have been "beatless".

The art versus the science

There is clearly not only one mistuning that can be said to "eliminate the beat". The reduction of beating to a minimum involves changes to beat rates, beat decay rates, fluctuation forms, and overall decay rates of partials. Whilst a given mistuning (as measured at the fundamental) may serve to attenuate beats in a large number of partials simultaneously, it will not necessarily attenuate beats in *all* partials simultaneously.

Different partials may require different mistunings for the best attenuation of their beating. When this is the case, the question arises *which* partials will be "compromised" and which ones will not? This is essentially where the art of tuning diverges from what the science can readily determine. The practical answer in each individual case lies in the perceived overall tone of the unison.

During the decay time, the tone can undergo changes and tonal "movement" that are not necessarily beating of the kind predicted by "traditional" theory. Aural tuners are of course adjusting this tone as an art, rather than carrying out digital analyses and making theory-based decisions.

Weakness in the *mistuning to improve decay time* hypothesis

There is also the question whether tuners introduce mistunings in order to improve unison decay time. The idea that tuners can adjust prompt sound and aftersound decay times *in a specific partial* is essentially correct, but it should be remembered there is a large number of partials contributing to the tone being adjusted.

In the analysis here, different partials have measurably different decay behaviour, and different decay rates, for a given mistuning between fundamentals. The argument for improved decay time would have to be made specifically for the longest decaying partial, which is not necessarily the fundamental.

In the analysis here, the longest decaying partial is the 2nd partial. Measurements from within the prompt sound to a level just above the noise floor, corresponding to a 33 dB fall, show different decay times. The slowest decay rates obtainable for the fundamental occur at the 3rd or 4th stages of tuning, when the decay pattern is a single null.

The decay time is then around 8.5 seconds, compared to just 3 seconds at the "optimum" tuning stage, or 5.2 seconds at stage 5. The problem with the *decay time hypothesis* here, is that *all* the other partials at this mistuning are actually *beating*, including those whose beating could be avoided. Aurally, the tuning at these stages is well outside the range in which the unison would be regarded as "good" by the professional tuner.

The 2nd partial, the longest decaying partial overall, does indeed have its longest decay time at the "optimum" tuning stage, where the decay time is 11.3 seconds, compared to 8.1 seconds at a tuning where the 2nd partial exhibits a "perfect" single null (no second beat appears on magnification), or 10.2 seconds at tuning stage 5.

This, at first sight, does make it look rather as though this supports the thesis that "optimum" tuning is one at which the decay time of the *longest decaying partial* is maximised. There are, however, two problems with this assertion.

Firstly, the decay rates of partials are only one adjustable feature of unison tone. The other major feature, which is in fact the *primary* feature of unison tone as far as the basic aural tuning remit is concerned, is *beating or fluctuations* in the partials. In the case in question, the decay time tuned for the 2nd partial - the partial that actually dominates the spectrum - is probably just a "side effect" of the mistuning chosen for the *other* partials, collectively.

74

This mistuning can be clearly observed to be the one that most reduces beating and fluctuations in the other partials, including reduction of false beating through attenuation.

Secondly, the mistuning (in the fundamental) at the point that maximises the decay time of the 2nd partial, is the one *closest to zero*, and which statistically might actually have been zero. When greater mistuning is introduced, the decay time actually *falls*, so its behaviour is definitely not consistent with the *decay time hypothesis*.

The notion that a unison will decay too fast at zero mistuning, relies on the presumption that the unison system is no more complicated than that described by the Weinreich 2X2 matrix theory, or as simple as that assumed in Benade's hypothesis. Both models (incorrectly) presume string motion in one plane only, and neither model would explain the existence of false beats, or double and multiple peaks for single partials in the spectral analyses of single strings.

Both models apply only to a single partial and do not describe the unison tone or behaviour as a whole, because they ignore the complexity of the whole system of partials that actually determine the tone.

The tone of the unison is affected by the fluctuations, amplitudes and decay rates of a large number of different partials. Many of these may have inherited "false beats", i.e. they contain fluctuations that are not affected by the mistuning in the same way that the other partials are.

In the final analysis the behaviour of individual strings and unisons is *highly diverse*, and study of any one string, only shows what *can* occur. Results from any one study are not necessarily a demonstration of universal behaviour. It is this sheer diversity and complication of behaviour that makes a fixed, "correct" mistuning value, impossible to assert on theoretical grounds alone.

False beat attenuation in the full trichord

The effect of the full trichord with respect to false beat attenuation, can be more pronounced. Fig. (12) compares a number of partials of the left hand single string with the corresponding partials of the full trichord of A49 on the same Steinway, aurally tuned to a "good" tuning.

Whilst the middle and right strings of the unison are not immediately noticeable as "false" to the casual ear, the left string is much more noticeably false. The vertical scales in each pair of graphs is equal, but the scales are not the same for all pairs – if they were, the shapes of the smallest amplitude partials would be difficult to discern. The time axes along the horizontal are all equal (0.7s units), so that the beat rates or speeds of fluctuations can be compared

Fig. 12

Single string partial   **Unison partial**

Partial 1

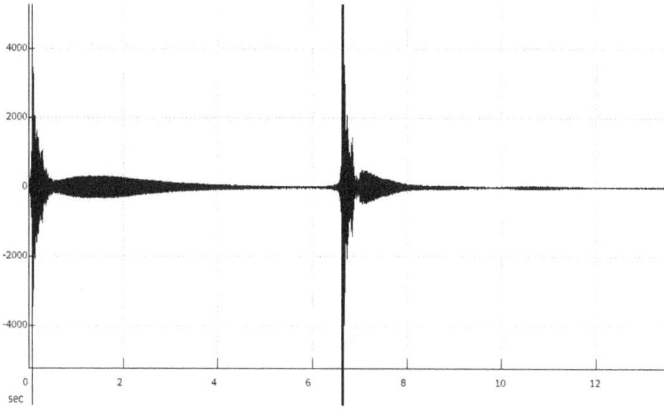

Partial 2

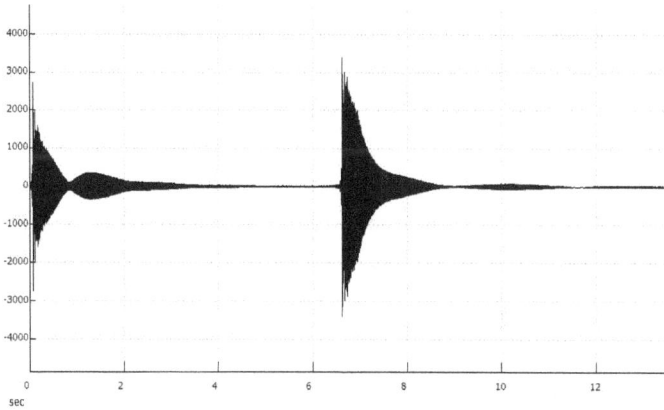

Partial 3

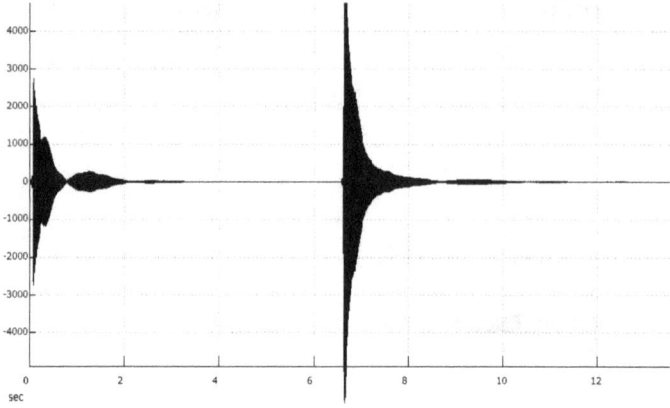

Partial 6

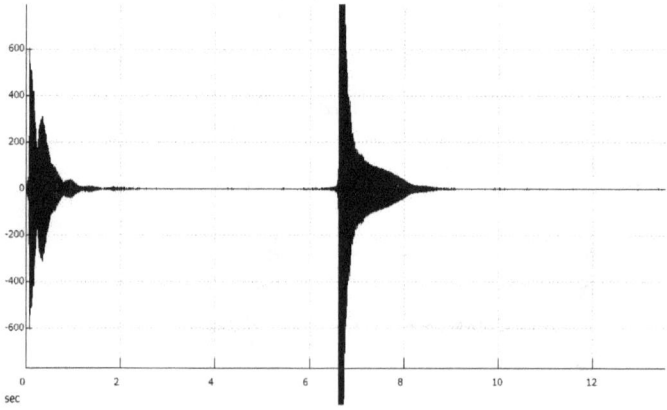

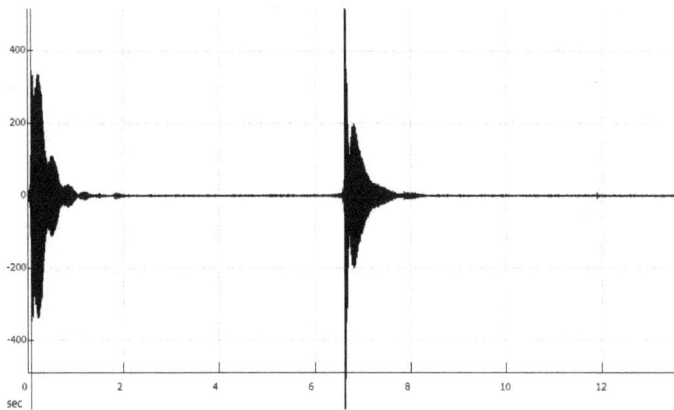

Partial 8

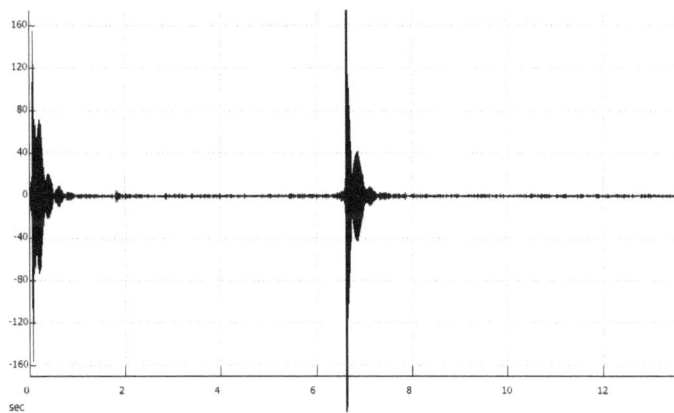

Partial 10

Partial 12

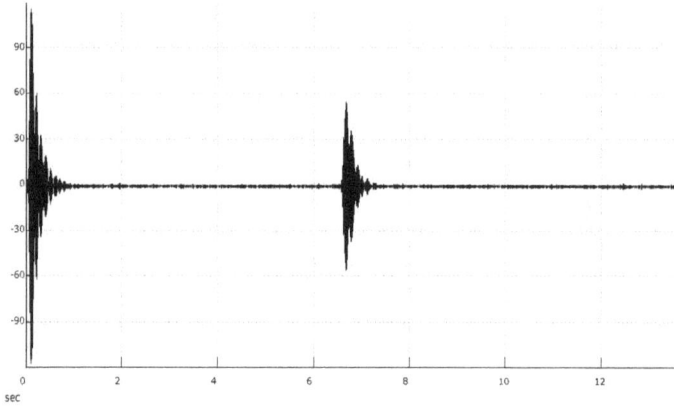

FFT frequency analysis of the unison

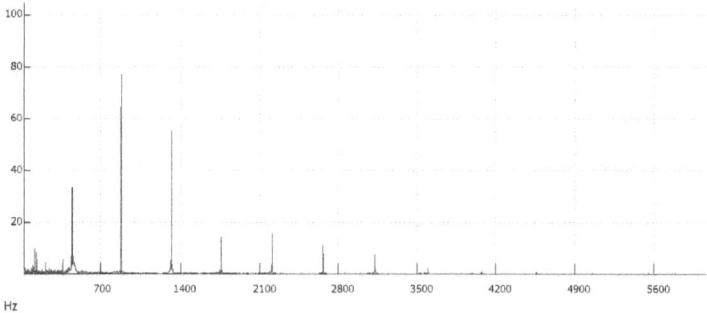

The frequency measurements of the trichord's fundamentals, sounding separately, are 438.49 Hz, 438.40 Hz and 438.57 Hz. The frequency resolution is ± 0.09 Hz. In 11 of the 12 cases the unison's partial is improved over the equivalent partial of the single string, in terms of attenuating fluctuations, for at least one of three reasons:

1. The false beat rate in the single string case is reduced in the unison.

2. The false beat amplitude (prominence) in the single string case is reduced in the unison.

3. The first null comes later in the decay, in the unison.

The unison partial number 12 decays more rapidly and appears to be initiated with a smaller amplitude.

The attenuation of false beat fluctuations in the way illustrated here, in the "optimum" tuning for a unison, is not inferred to be a universal rule for all partials, in all unisons, from these results. It is also possible to find cases where there is no attenuation or a faster beat rate in the unison than in the single string.

The trichord system is very complicated in this respect, because up to all three strings may be false at a given partial number, in different ways, and from different physical parameter configurations. The results for unisons do in general, however, seem to show that this attenuation "mechanism" is a prominent feature.

Conclusion

The theoretical models

"Traditional" piano tuning theory is based on a simple theoretical model that cannot accurately describe what happens in fine unison tuning. The Weinreich 2X2 matrix theory for two unison strings in one plane is itself also an idealised theory, but one that gives much more insight into unison behaviour than the "traditional" piano tuning theory.

A somewhat more "realistic" modelling of the two-string unison system can be carried out by using a 4X4 matrix that allows for motion in two planes, and also allows for anisotropic boundary conditions at the bridge – this models for the presence of the "false beat" phenomena that is an everyday reality in tuning practice.

"False beat" phenomena is not limited to those instances that piano tuners would immediately recognise. It is a ubiquitous aspect of piano tone that affects tuning even when not overtly recognised. Real piano string audible partials demonstrably can contain two or more close-frequency components, that can lead to "false beat" pattern formation in the partial decay.

Whilst it is only the more extreme or prominent cases of this phenomena that many tuners refer to as "false beats", the phenomena nonetheless exists at a lesser degree as a natural part of normal piano string behaviour. Other causes of "false beat" phenomena may exist, but this possibility does not itself invalidate the anisotropic boundary model.

The generalisation of the matrix theory predicts this, digital analysis demonstrates it, and piano tuners deal with it on an everyday basis, even on the best instruments without necessarily even realising it.

The 4X4 matrix theory, so configured, can generate results in which the least fluctuation occurs when there is a mistuning between the strings, rather than at zero mistuning. Actual measurements of unison string frequencies show instances of mistunings occurring between strings of the well tuned unison, as well as instances where mistuning is very close to zero (or perhaps zero).

The *improved decay time hypothesis*

It has often been supposed that tuners may introduce mistuning between unison strings in order to "improve decay time". Mistunings in unisons tuned by expert aural tuners cannot satisfactorily be explained simply as a means of increasing unison decay time in the aftersound.

This hypothesis (a) neglects the presence and effect of multiple partials; (b) does not recognise coupled string motion in two planes; (c) is not consistently observable in practice, whether applied to the fundamental, the most prominent partial, or the longest decaying partial.

Mistuning variations

In the central compass there appears (from Kirk) to be a mistuning range of perhaps 1 - 2 cents inside which any mistuning may result in an acceptable unison to the ears of musicians. A possible objective counterpart of this, is that within this limited range, partials that are capable of becoming entirely beatless (i.e. the corresponding partials in the single strings are not false), are either beatless or in a singe null decay pattern, over the whole range. However, in the central compass mistuning changes of around 1/3 cent and possibly less, can still create aurally significant changes to the soundscape that the professional tuner would take into account in adjusting the tone of the unison.

These changes are associated with observable changes to partials that are not themselves capable of becoming entirely beatless (i.e. the corresponding partials in the single strings are slightly false). These ranges apply to the high quality instrument.

There are a large number of parameters affecting the tuning behaviour of a unison pair. In the matrix theory model for the unison pair in two planes there are 16 such parameters, and a correspondingly much larger number of combinations of parameter values and relationships. Thus, for a unison pair, there is unlikely to be a fixed mistuning for giving an "optimum" tuning, for all unisons. Results for one or two unisons cannot be inductively applied to all unisons.

Trichords

Trichord behaviour is even more complicated. Dual decay rates can be observed for trichords, but the Benade hypothesis for explaining prompt sound and aftersound in the trichord ignores coupled motion in two planes. The matrix representation for the trichord in two planes contains 36 parameters and a correspondingly much larger number of combinations of parameter values and relationships. Some principles broadly similar to those that the Weinreich matrix generates, can be observed in the relationship between mistuning and decay curves, in the matrix for the full trichord in two planes. However, the overall situation is much more complicated.

There seems potentially to be some indication that the reactive part of the bridge admittance in the theoretical model, may even cause complex chaotic behaviour in the trichord's frequencies and decay rates. This has been indicated by the presence of bifurcation in the graphs generated. Whilst this could be an obscure computational artefact, it could also be that the model is correctly indicating that three-string unison behaviour is inherently unpredictable.

In reducing beat rates, it is not only the reduction of beat rate that causes beat attenuation. In both theory and empirical analysis, beat amplitudes in general, may decay at different rates to the overall partial decay rate, which itself may not be constant.

As the beat rate is reduced, the beat decay rate also assists in attenuating the beat by progressively reducing its amplitude. In general, in the process of reducing an "adjustable" beat rate in the unison, where no "false" phenomena are present in the single string partials, a beat typically reduces first to a single null form, and then to a dual decay rate, and finally to a straightforward exponential decay.

The art beyond "tuning out the beat"

A statement that master tuners tune unisons by "tuning out the beat", is arguably better than saying that strings are being "tuned to the same pitch". Nevertheless, both ideas are misleadingly oversimplified.

Certainly, in learning to tune, there are stages at which each notion necessarily might suffice, but there is little in the contemporary theory or in empirical scientific observation, to support the notion that this part of the art of tuning can be reduced to such simple conceptual terms.

The notion that issues of unison tuning can be reduced to one of accuracy measured in cents, compared to some pre-defined "perfect" value, is essentially incorrect. No tuners with proper training and reasonable skill, fine tune unisons by pitch, and the cent is not in any case a valid measurement of micro-pitch for piano tone.

The optimum tone and tuning condition for all unisons is not necessarily at zero mistuning. There may be a range of mistunings over which the "beat" in a given partial is "eliminated".

Different mistunings in this range may alter the tonal recipe, primarily by altering the decay patterns of what are essentially "false" partials, and decay rates in general. Furthermore, the mistuning required to eliminate or attenuate beating is not necessarily the same for all partials. Whilst this effect is rather obvious in the tuning of covered bass strings, it is also present in the plain steel string trichords.

From the expert aural tuner's point of view, the art of tuning is about the production of tone and intonation and the optimising of the sonic, musical qualities of the instrument, through the unisons, the intervals they form, and the relationship of one part of the compass to another. As far as the unison itself is concerned, it could be said that "inside" pitch similarity between the strings, is an area of tone control through a process that has been called "eliminating the beat".

This is in actuality the reduction of a multiplicity of different beat rates. "Inside" this, is a further area of tone control in which the artist tuner works as a matter everyday practice.

Here, in technical terms, it seems likely that what is going on is not so much the reducing of adjustable beat *rates*, but the *attenuation* of "false" beat patterns, single null patterns, and other essentially "false" fluctuations, together with the critical adjustment of partial decay rates, in a complex recipe of ingredients determining the tone.

References

Benade, AH, *Fundamentals of musical acoustics*, NY, 1976, p. 336

Braid White, W, *Piano Tuning and Allied Arts*, 1917, 14th reprint 1972, p. 106

Campbell, M, & Greated, C, *The musician's guide to acoustics*, London, 1987

Capleton, B, 'False beats in coupled piano string unisons', *JASA*, 115 (2), 2004, 885-892

Cartling, Bo, 'Frequency and amplitude modulation of the piano tone due to coupling of tones', *JASA*, April 2005, 117, 4, pp. 2259-2267

Chase Hundley, T, Benioff, H, and Martin, DW, 'Factors contributing to the multiple rate of piano tone decay', *JASA*, 64,5, 1973, pp. 1303-1309

Kirk, RE, 'Tuning Preferences for Piano Unison Groups',
JASA, 31, 1959, pp. 1644–1648

Martin, DW, 'Decay rates of piano tones', *JASA*, 19,4, 1947,
pp. 535-541

Martin, DW, and Ward, WD, 'Subjective Evaluation of
Musical Scale Temperament in Pianos' *JASA*, 26, 1954, 932;
33, 1962, pp. 582-585

Weinreich, G, 'Coupled piano tones', *JASA*, 62, 6, 1977, pp.
1474-1484